CATHOLIC SUNDAY AND DAILY MASS READINGS

For OCTOBER 2024

[Book 10 of 12]

Catholic Missal, Lectionary with Celebrations of the Liturgical Year 2024 [Year B]

Dear Reader,

Thank you for purchasing and reading this book.

I sincerely thank you for your trust. Let us pray together and invite our Lord in Heaven into everyday life.

If you like this book, please don't hesitate to tell your friends and family about it so that more people can benefit. Thank you again for your support, and happy reading.

May our Savior be glorified, and may He bless you. Amen.

CONTENTS

PART I

a. PRINCIPAL CELEBRATIONS OF THE LITURGICAL YEAR B, 2024

CELEBRATIONS	DATE
First Sunday of Advent, Year B	December 3, 2023
Ash Wednesday	February 14, 2024
Easter Sunday	March 31, 2024
The Ascension of the Lord (Sunday)	May 12, 2024
Pentecost Sunday	May 19, 2024
The Most Holy Body and Blood of Christ (Corpus Christi)	June 2, 2024
First Sunday of Advent, Year C	December 1, 2024

b. CYCLES - LECTIONARY FOR MASS

Sunday Cycle	Year B	December 3, 2023 to November 24, 2024
Weekday Cycle	Cycle II	January 9 to February 13, 2024 May 20 to November 30, 2024
Sunday Cycle	Year C	December 1, 2024 to November 23, 2025

PART II

SUNDAY AND DAILY MASS READINGS 2024

OCTOBER 2024

October 1, 2024

Memorial of Saint Thérèse of the Child Jesus, virgin and doctor of the Church

First Reading: Job 3: 1-3, 11-17, 20-23

1 After this Job opened his mouth, and cursed his day,*2* And he said:*3* Let the day perish wherein I was born, and the night in which it was said: A man child is conceived.

11 Why did I not die in the womb, why did I not perish when I came out of the belly?*12* Why received upon the knees? why suckled at the breasts?*13* For now I should have been asleep and still, and should have rest in my sleep.*14* With kings and consuls of the earth, who build themselves solitudes:*15* Or with princes, that possess gold, and All their houses with silver:*16* Or as a hidden untimely birth I should not be, or as they that being conceived have not seen the light.*17* There the wicked cease from tumult, and there the wearied in strength are at rest.

20 Why is light given to him that is in misery, and life to them that are in bitterness of soul?*21* That look for death, and it cometh not, as they that dig for a treasure:*22* And they rejoice exceedingly when they have found the grave.*23* To a man whose way is hidden, and God hath surrounded him with darkness?

Responsorial Psalm: Psalms 88: 2-3, 4-5, 6, 7-8

R. (3) Let my prayer come before you, Lord.

2 O Lord, the God of my salvation: I have cried in the day, and in the night before thee.

3 Let my prayer come in before thee: incline thy ear to my petition.

R. Let my prayer come before you, Lord.

4 For my soul is filled with evils: and my life hath drawn nigh to hell.

5 I am counted among them that go down to the pit: I am become as a man without help,

R. Let my prayer come before you, Lord.

6 Free among the dead. Like the slain sleeping in the sepulchres, whom thou rememberest no more: and they are cast off from thy hand.

R. Let my prayer come before you, Lord.

7 They have laid me in the lower pit: in the dark places, and in the shadow of death.

8 Thy wrath is strong over me: and all thy waves thou hast brought in upon me.

R. Let my prayer come before you, Lord.

Alleluia: Mark 10: 45

R. Alleluia, alleluia.

45 The Son of Man came to serve and to give his life as a ransom for many.

R. Alleluia, alleluia.

Gospel: Luke 9: 51-56

51 And it came to pass, when the days of his assumption were accomplishing, that he steadfastly set his face to go to Jerusalem.*52* And he sent messengers before his face; and going, they entered into a city of the Samaritans, to prepare for him.*53* And they received him not, because his face was of one going to Jerusalem.*54* And when his disciples James and John had seen this, they said: Lord, wilt thou that we command fire to come down from heaven, and consume them?*55* And turning, he rebuked them, saying: You know not of what spirit you are.*56* The Son of man came not to destroy souls, but to save. And they went into another town.

October 2, 2024

Memorial of the Holy Guardian Angels

First Reading: Job 9: 1-12, 14-16

1 And Job answered, and said:*2* Indeed I know it is so, and that man cannot be justified compared with God.*3* If he will contend with him, he cannot answer him one for a thousand.*4* He is wise in heart, and mighty in strength: who hath resisted him, and hath had peace?*5* Who hath removed mountains, and they whom he overthrew in his wrath, knew it not.*6* Who shaketh the earth out of her place, and the pillars thereof tremble.*7* Who commandeth tile sun and it riseth not: and shutteth up the stars as it were under a seal:*8* Who alone spreadeth out the heavens, and walketh upon the waves of the sea.*9* Who maketh Arcturus, and Orion, and Hyades, and the inner parts of the south.*10* Who doth things great and incomprehensible, and wonderful, of which there is no number. *11* If he come to me, I shall not see him: if he depart I shall not understand. *12* If he examine on a sudden, who shall answer him? or who can say: Why dost thou so? *14* What am I then, that I should answer him, and have words with him? *15* I, who although I should have any just thing, would not answer, but would make supplication to my judge. *16* And if he should hear me when I call, I should not believe that he had heard my voice.

Responsorial Psalm: Psalms 88: 10bc-11, 12-13, 14-15

R. (3) Let my prayer come before you, Lord.

10bc All the day I cried to thee, O Lord: I stretched out my hands to thee.

11 Wilt thou shew wonders to the dead? or shall physicians raise to life, and give praise to thee?

R. Let my prayer come before you, Lord.

12 Shall any one in the sepulchre declare thy mercy: and thy truth in destruction?

13 Shall thy wonders be known in the dark; and thy justice in the land of forgetfulness?

R. Let my prayer come before you, Lord.

14 But I, O Lord, have cried to thee: and in the morning my prayer shall prevent thee.

15 Lord, why castest thou off my prayer: why turnest thou away thy face from me?

R. Let my prayer come before you, Lord.

Alleluia: Psalms 103: 21

R. Alleluia, alleluia.

21 Bless the LORD, all you angels, you ministers, who do his will.

R. Alleluia, alleluia.

Gospel: Matthew 18: 1-5, 10

1 At that hour the disciples came to Jesus, saying: Who thinkest thou is the greater in the kingdom of heaven?*2* And Jesus calling unto him a little child, set him in the midst of them,*3* And said: Amen I say to you, unless you be converted, and become as little children, you shall not enter into the kingdom of heaven.*4* Whosoever therefore shall humble himself as this little child, he is the greater in the kingdom of heaven.*5* And he that shall receive one such little child in my name, receiveth me.*10* See that you despise not one of these little ones: for I say to you, that their angels in heaven always see the face of my Father who is in heaven.

October 3, 2024

Thursday of the Twenty-sixth Week in Ordinary Time

First Reading: Job 19: 21-27

21 Have pity on me, have pity on me, at least you my friends, because the hand of the Lord hath touched me.*22* Why do you persecute me as God, and glut yourselves with my flesh?*23* Who will grant me that my words may be written? Who will grant me that they may be marked down in a book?*24* With an iron pen and in a plate of lead, or else be graven with an instrument in flint stone.*25* For I know that my Redeemer liveth, and in the last day I shall rise out of the earth.*26* And I shall be clothed again with my skin, and in my flesh I will see my God.*27* Whom I myself shall see, and my eyes shall behold, and not another: this my hope is laid up in my bosom.

Responsorial Psalm: Psalms 27: 7-8a, 8b-9abc, 13-14

R. (13) I believe that I shall see the good things of the Lord in the land of the living.

7 Hear, O Lord, my voice, with which I have cried to thee: have mercy on me and hear me.

8a My heart hath said to thee: My face hath sought thee.

R. I believe that I shall see the good things of the Lord in the land of the living.

8b, 9abc Thy face, O Lord, will I still seek. Turn not away thy face from me; decline not in thy wrath from thy servant. Be thou my helper, forsake me not.

R. I believe that I shall see the good things of the Lord in the land of the living.

13 I believe to see the good things of the Lord in the land of the living.

14 Expect the Lord, do manfully, and let thy heart take courage, and wait thou for the Lord.

R. I believe that I shall see the good things of the Lord in the land of the living.

Alleluia: Mark 1: 15

R. Alleluia, alleluia.

15 The Kingdom of God is at hand; repent and believe in the Gospel.

R. Alleluia, alleluia.

Gospel: Luke 10: 1-12

1 And after these things the Lord appointed also other seventy-two: and he sent them two and two before his face into every city and place whither he himself was to come.*2* And he said to them: The harvest indeed is great, but the labourers are few. Pray ye therefore the Lord of the harvest, that he send labourers into his harvest.*3* Go: Behold I send you as lambs among wolves.*4* Carry neither purse, nor scrip, nor shoes; and salute no man by the way.*5* Into whatsoever house you enter, first say: Peace be to this house.*6* And if the son of peace be there, your peace shall rest upon him; but if not, it shall return to you.*7* And in the same house, remain, eating and drinking such things as they have: for the labourer is worthy of his hire. Remove not from house to house.*8* And into what city soever you enter, and they receive you, eat such things as are set before you.*9* And heal the sick that are therein, and say to them: The kingdom of God is come nigh unto you.*10* But into whatsoever city you enter, and they receive you not, going forth into the streets thereof, say:*11* Even the very dust of your city that cleaveth to us, we wipe off against you. Yet know this, that the kingdom of God is at hand.*12* I say to you, it shall be more tolerable at that day for Sodom, than for that city.

October 4, 2024

Memorial of Saint Francis of Assisi

First Reading: Job 38: 1, 12-21; 40: 3-5

1 Then the Lord answered Job out of a whirlwind, and said:*12* Didst thou since thy birth command the morning, and shew the dawning of the day its place?*13* And didst thou hold the extremities of the earth shaking them, and hast thou shaken the ungodly out of it?*14* The seal shall be restored as clay, and shall stand as a garment:*15* From the wicked their light shall be taken away, and the high arm shall be broken.*16* Hast thou entered into the depths of the sea, and walked in the lowest parts of the deep?*17* Have the gates of death been opened to thee, and hast thou seen the darksome doors?*18* Hast thou considered the breadth of the earth? tell me, if thou knowest all things?*19* Where is the way where light dwelleth, and where is the place of darkness:*20* That thou mayst bring every thing to its own bounds, and understand the paths of the house thereof.*21* Didst thou know then that thou shouldst be born? and didst thou know the number of thy days?*40:3* Then Job answered the Lord, and said:*4* What can I answer, who hath spoken inconsiderately? I will lay my hand upon my mouth.*5* One thing I have spoken, which I wish I had not said: and another, to which I will add no more.

Responsorial Psalm: Psalms 139: 1-3, 7-8, 9-10, 13-14ab

R. (24b) Guide me, Lord, along the everlasting way.

1 Lord, thou hast proved me, and known me:

2 Thou hast know my sitting down, and my rising up.

3 Thou hast understood my thoughts afar off: my path and my line thou hast searched out.

R. Guide me, Lord, along the everlasting way.

7 Whither shall I go from thy spirit? or whither shall I flee from thy face?

8 If I ascend into heaven, thou art there: if I descend into hell, thou art present.

R. Guide me, Lord, along the everlasting way.

9 If I take my wings early in the morning, and dwell in the uttermost parts of the sea:

10 Even there also shall thy hand lead me: and thy right hand shall hold me.

R. Guide me, Lord, along the everlasting way.

13 For thou hast possessed my reins: thou hast protected me from my mother's womb.

14 I will praise thee, for thou art fearfully magnified: wonderful are thy works.

R. Guide me, Lord, along the everlasting way.

Alleluia: Psalms 95: 8

R. Alleluia, alleluia.

8 If today you hear his voice, harden not your hearts.

R. Alleluia, alleluia.

Gospel: Luke 10: 13-16

13 Woe to thee, Corozain, woe to thee, Bethsaida. For if in Tyre and Sidon had been wrought the mighty works that have been wrought in you, they would have done penance long ago, sitting in sackcloth and ashes.14 But it shall be more tolerable for Tyre and Sidon at the judgement, than for you.15 And thou, Capharnaum, which art exalted unto heaven, thou shalt be thrust down to hell.16 He that heareth you, heareth me; and he that despiseth you, despiseth me; and he that despiseth me, despiseth him that sent me.

October 5, 2024

Saturday of the Twenty-sixth Week in Ordinary Time

First Reading: Job 42: 1-3, 5-6, 12-17

1 Then Job answered the Lord, and said:2 I know that thou canst do all things, and no thought is hid from thee.3 Who is this that hideth counsel without knowledge?

Therefore I have spoken unwisely, and things that above measure exceeded my knowledge.*5* With the hearing of the ear, I have heard thee, but now my eye seeth thee.*6* Therefore I reprehend myself, and do penance in dust and ashes.*12* And the Lord blessed the latter end of Job more than his beginning. And he had fourteen thousand sheep, and six thousand camels, and a thousand yoke of oxen, and a thousand she asses.*13* And he had seven sons, and three daughters.*14* And he called the names of one Dies, and the name of the second Cassia, and the name of the third Cornustibil.*15* And there were not found in all the earth women so beautiful as the daughters of Job: and their father gave them inheritance among their brethren.*16* And Job lived after these things, a hundred and forty years, and he saw his children, and his children's children, unto the fourth generation,*17* and he died an old man, and full of days.

Responsorial Psalm: Psalms 119: 66, 71, 75, 91, 125, 130

R. (135) Lord, let your face shine on me.

66 Teach me goodness and discipline and knowledge; for I have believed thy commandments.

R. Lord, let your face shine on me.

71 It is good for me that thou hast humbled me, that I may learn thy justifications.

R. Lord, let your face shine on me.

75 I know, O Lord, that thy judgments are equity: and in thy truth thou hast humbled me.

R. Lord, let your face shine on me.

91 By thy ordinance the day goeth on: for all things serve thee.

R. Lord, let your face shine on me.

125 I am thy servant: give me understanding that I may know thy testimonies.

R. Lord, let your face shine on me.

130 The declaration of thy words giveth light: and giveth understanding to little ones.

R. Lord, let your face shine on me.

Alleluia: Matthew 11: 25

R. Alleluia, alleluia.

25 Blessed are you, Father, Lord of heaven and earth, you have revealed to little ones the mysteries of the Kingdom.

R. Alleluia, alleluia.

Gospel: Luke 10: 17-24

17 And the seventy-two returned with joy, saying: Lord, the devils also are subject to us in thy name.*18* And he said to them: I saw Satan like lightning falling from heaven.*19* Behold, I have given you power to tread upon serpents and scorpions, and upon all the power of the enemy: and nothing shall hurt you.*20* But yet rejoice not in this, that spirits are subject unto you; but rejoice in this, that your names are written in heaven.*21* In that same hour, he rejoiced in the Holy Ghost, and said: I confess to thee, O Father, Lord of heaven and earth, because thou hast hidden these things from the wise and prudent, and hast revealed them to little ones. Yea, Father, for so it hath seemed good in thy sight.*22* All things are delivered to me by my Father; and no one knoweth who the Son is, but the Father; and who the Father is, but the Son, and to whom the Son will reveal him.*23* And turning to his disciples, he said: Blessed are the eyes that see the things which you see.*24* For I say to you, that many prophets and kings have desired to see the things that you see, and have not seen them; and to hear the things that you hear, and have not heard them.

October 6, 2024

Twenty-seventh Sunday in Ordinary Time

First Reading: Genesis 2: 18-24

18 And the Lord God said: It is not good for man to be alone: let us make him a help like unto himself.*19* And the Lord God having formed out of the ground all the beasts of the earth, and all the fowls of the air, brought them to Adam to see what he would call them: for whatsoever Adam called any living creature the same is its name.*20* And Adam called all the beasts by their names, and all the fowls of the air, and all the cattle of the field: but for Adam there was not found a helper like himself.*21* Then the Lord God cast a deep sleep upon Adam: and when he was fast asleep, he took one of his ribs, and filled up flesh for it.*22* And the Lord God built the rib which he took from Adam into a woman: and brought her to Adam.*23* And Adam said: This now is bone of my bones, and flesh of my flesh; she shall be called woman, because she was taken out of man.*24* Wherefore a man shall leave father and mother, and shall cleave to his wife: and they shall be two in one flesh.

Responsorial Psalm: Psalms 128: 1-2, 3, 4-5, 6

R. (5) May the Lord bless us all the days of our lives.

1 Blessed are all they that fear the Lord: that walk in his ways.

2 For thou shalt eat the labours of thy hands: blessed art thou, and it shall be well with thee.

R. May the Lord bless us all the days of our lives.

3 Thy wife as a fruitful vine, on the sides of thy house.

R. May the Lord bless us all the days of our lives.

4 Behold, thus shall the man be blessed that feareth the Lord.

5 May the Lord bless thee out of Sion: and mayest thou see the good things of Jerusalem all the days of thy life.

R. May the Lord bless us all the days of our lives.

6 And mayest thou see thy children's children, peace upon Israel.

R. May the Lord bless us all the days of our lives.

Second Reading: Hebrews 2: 9-11

9 But we see Jesus, who was made a little lower than the angels, for the suffering of death, crowned with glory and honour: that, through the grace of God, he might taste death for all.*10* For it became him, for whom are all things, and by whom are all things, who had brought many children into glory, to perfect the author of their salvation, by his passion.*11* For both he that sanctifieth, and they who are sanctified, are all of one. For which cause he is not ashamed to call them brethren, saying:

Alleluia: First John 4: 12

R. Alleluia, alleluia.

12 If we love one another, God remains in us and his love is brought to perfection in us.

R. Alleluia, alleluia.

Gospel: Mark 10: 2-16

2 And the Pharisees coming to him asked him: Is it lawful for a man to put away his wife? tempting him.*3* But he answering, saith to them: What did Moses command you?*4* Who said: Moses permitted to write a bill of divorce, and to put her away.*5* To whom Jesus answering, said: Because of the hardness of your heart he wrote you that precept.*6* But from the beginning of the creation, God made them male and female.*7* For this cause a man shall leave his father and mother; and shall cleave to his wife.*8* And they two shall be in one flesh. Therefore now they are not two, but one flesh.*9* What therefore God hath joined together, let not man put asunder.*10* And in the house again his disciples asked him concerning the same thing.*11* And he saith to them: Whosoever shall put away his wife and marry another, committeth adultery against her.*12* And if the wife shall put away her husband, and be married to another, she committeth adultery.*13* And they brought to him young children, that he might touch them. And the disciples rebuked them that brought them.*14* Whom when Jesus saw, he was much displeased, and saith to them: Suffer the little children to come unto me, and forbid them not; for of such is the kingdom of God.*15* Amen I say to you, whosoever shall not receive the kingdom of God as a little child, shall not enter into it.*16* And embracing them, and laying his hands upon them, he blessed them.

October 7, 2024

Memorial of Our Lady of the Rosary

First Reading: Galatians 1: 6-12

6 I wonder that you are so soon removed from him that called you into the grace of Christ, unto another gospel.*7* Which is not another, only there are some that trouble you, and would pervert the gospel of Christ.*8* But though we, or an angel from heaven, preach a gospel to you besides that which we have preached to you, let him be anathema.*9* As we said before, so now I say again: If any one preach to you a gospel, besides that which you have received, let him be anathema.*10* For do I now persuade men, or God? Or do I seek to please men? If I yet pleased men, I should not be the servant of Christ.*11* For I give you to understand, brethren, that the gospel which was preached by me is not according to man.*12* For neither did I receive it of man, nor did I learn it; but by the revelation of Jesus Christ.

Responsorial Psalm: Psalms 111: 1b-2, 7-8, 9 and 10c

R. (5) The Lord will remember his covenant for ever.

or

R. Alleluia.

1 I will praise thee, O Lord, with my whole heart; in the council of the just: and in the congregation.

2 Great are the works of the Lord: sought out according to all his wills.

R. The Lord will remember his covenant for ever.

or

R. Alleluia.

7 That he may give them the inheritance of the Gentiles: the works of his hands are truth and judgment.

8 All his commandments are faithful: confirmed for ever and ever, made in truth and equity.

R. The Lord will remember his covenant for ever.

or

R. Alleluia.

9 He hath sent redemption to his people: he hath commanded his covenant for ever. Holy and terrible is his name:

10c His praise continueth for ever and ever.

R. The Lord will remember his covenant for ever.

or

R. Alleluia.

Alleluia: John 13: 34

R. Alleluia, alleluia.

34 I give you a new commandment: love one another as I have loved you.

R. Alleluia, alleluia.

Gospel: Luke 10: 25-37

25 And behold a certain lawyer stood up, tempting him, and saying, Master, what must I do to possess eternal life?26 But he said to him: What is written in the law? how readest thou?27 He answering, said: Thou shalt love the Lord thy God with thy whole heart, and with thy whole soul, and with all thy strength, and with all thy mind: and thy neighbour as thyself.28 And he said to him: Thou hast answered right: this do, and thou shalt live.29 But he willing to justify himself, said to Jesus: And who is my neighbour?30 And Jesus answering, said: A certain man went down from Jerusalem to Jericho, and fell among robbers, who also stripped him, and having wounded him went away, leaving him half dead.31 And it chanced, that a certain priest went down the same way: and seeing him, passed by.32 In like manner also a Levite, when he was near the place and saw him, passed by.33 But a certain Samaritan being on his journey, came near him; and seeing him, was moved with compassion.34 And going up to him, bound up his wounds, pouring in oil and wine: and setting him upon his own beast, brought him to an inn, and took care of him.35 And the next day he took out two pence, and gave to the host, and said: Take care of him; and whatsoever thou shalt spend over and above, I, at my return, will repay thee.36 Which of these three, in thy opinion, was neighbour to him that fell among the robbers?37 But he said: He that shewed mercy to him. And Jesus said to him: Go, and do thou in like manner.

October 8, 2024

Tuesday of the Twenty-seventh Week in Ordinary Time

First Reading: Galatians 1: 13-24

13 For you have heard of my conversation in time past in the Jews' religion: how that, beyond measure, I persecuted the church of God, and wasted it.14 And I made progress in the Jews' religion above many of my equals in my own nation, being more abundantly zealous for the traditions of my fathers.15 But when it pleased him,

who separated me from my mother's womb, and called me by his grace,*16* To reveal his Son in me, that I might preach him among the Gentiles, immediately I condescended not to flesh and blood.*17* Neither went I to Jerusalem, to the apostles who were before me: but I went into Arabia, and again I returned to Damascus.*18* Then, after three years, I went to Jerusalem, to see Peter, and I tarried with him fifteen days.*19* But other of the apostles I saw none, saving James the brother of the Lord.*20* Now the things which I write to you, behold, before God, I lie not.*21* Afterwards I came into the regions of Syria and Cilicia.*22* And I was unknown by face to the churches of Judea, which were in Christ:*23* But they had heard only: He, who persecuted us in times past, doth now preach the faith which once he impugned:*24* And they glorified God in me.

Responsorial Psalm: Psalms 139: 1b-3, 13-14ab, 14c-15

R. (24b) Guide me, Lord, along the everlasting way.

1 Lord, thou hast proved me, and known me:

2 Thou hast know my sitting down, and my rising up.

3 Thou hast understood my thoughts afar off: my path and my line thou hast searched out.

R. Guide me, Lord, along the everlasting way.

13 For thou hast possessed my reins: thou hast protected me from my mother's womb.

14ab I will praise thee, for thou art fearfully magnified: wonderful are thy works.

R. Guide me, Lord, along the everlasting way.

14c My soul knoweth right well.

15 My bone is not hidden from thee, which thou hast made in secret: and my substance in the lower parts of the earth.

R. Guide me, Lord, along the everlasting way.

Alleluia: Luke 11: 28

R. Alleluia, alleluia.

28 Blessed are those who hear the word of God and observe it.

R. Alleluia, alleluia.

Gospel: Luke 10: 38-42

38 Now it came to pass as they went, that he entered into a certain town: and a certain woman named Martha, received him into her house.*39* And she had a sister called Mary, who sitting also at the Lord's feet, heard his word.*40* But Martha was busy about much serving. Who stood and said: Lord, hast thou no care that my sister hath left me alone to serve? speak to her therefore, that she help me.*41* And the Lord answering, said to her: Martha, Martha, thou art careful, and art troubled about many things:*42* But one thing is necessary. Mary hath chosen the best part, which shall not be taken away from her.

October 9, 2024

Wednesday of the Twenty-seventh Week in Ordinary Time

First Reading: Galatians 2: 1-2, 7-14

1 Then, after fourteen years, I went up again to Jerusalem with Barnabas, taking Titus also with me.*2* And I went up according to revelation; and communicated to them the gospel, which I preach among the Gentiles, but apart to them who seemed to be some thing: lest perhaps I should run, or had run in vain.*7* But contrariwise, when they had seen that to me was committed the gospel of the uncircumcision, as to Peter was that of the circumcision.*8* (For he who wrought in Peter to the apostleship of the circumcision, wrought in me also among the Gentiles.)*9* And when they had known the grace that was given to me, James and Cephas and John, who seemed to be pillars, gave to me and Barnabas the right hands of fellowship: that we should go unto the Gentiles, and they unto the circumcision:*10* Only that we should be mindful of the poor: which same thing also I was careful to do.*11* But when Cephas was come to Antioch, I withstood him to the face, because he was to be blamed.*12* For before that some came from James, he did eat with the Gentiles: but when they were come, he withdrew and separated himself, fearing them who were of the circumcision.*13* And to his dissimulation the rest of the Jews consented, so that Barnabas also was led by them into that dissimulation.*14* But when I saw that they walked not uprightly unto the truth of the gospel, I said to Cephas before them all: If thou, being a Jew, livest after the manner of the Gentiles, and not as the Jews do, how dost thou compel the Gentiles to live as do the Jews?

Responsorial Psalm: Psalms 117: 1bc, 2

R. Go out to all the world, and tell the Good News.

1 O praise the Lord, all ye nations: praise him, all ye people.

R. Go out to all the world, and tell the Good News.

2 For his mercy is confirmed upon us: and the truth of the Lord remaineth for ever.

R. Go out to all the world, and tell the Good News.

Alleluia: Romans 8: 15bc

R. Alleluia, alleluia.

15bc You have received a spirit of adoption as sons through which we cry: Abba! Father!

R. Alleluia, alleluia.

Gospel: Luke 11: 1-4

1 And it came to pass, that as he was in a certain place praying, when he ceased, one of his disciples said to him: Lord, teach us to pray, as John also taught his disciples.*2* And he said to them: When you pray, say: Father, hallowed be thy name. Thy kingdom come.*3* Give us this day our daily bread.*4* And forgive us our sins, for we also forgive every one that is indebted to us. And lead us not into temptation.

October 10, 2024

Thursday of the Twenty-seventh Week in Ordinary Time

First Reading: Galatians 3: 1-5

1 O senseless Galatians, who hath bewitched you that you should not obey the truth, before whose eyes Jesus Christ hath been set forth, crucified among you?*2* This only would I learn of you: Did you receive the Spirit by the works of the law, or by the hearing of faith?*3* Are you so foolish, that, whereas you began in the Spirit, you would now be made perfect by the flesh?*4* Have you suffered so great things in vain? If it be yet in vain.*5* He therefore who giveth to you the Spirit, and worketh miracles among you; doth he do it by the works of the law, or by the hearing of the faith?

Responsorial Psalm: Luke 1: 69, 70-71, 72, 73-75

R. (68) Blessed be the Lord, the God of Israel; he has come to his people.

69 And hath raised up an horn of salvation to us, in the house of David his servant:

R. Blessed be the Lord, the God of Israel; he has come to his people.

70 As he spoke by the mouth of his holy prophets, who are from the beginning:

71 Salvation from our enemies, and from the hand of all that hate us.

R. Blessed be the Lord, the God of Israel; he has come to his people.

72 To perform mercy to our fathers, and to remember his holy testament,

R. Blessed be the Lord, the God of Israel; he has come to his people.

73 The oath, which he swore to Abraham our father, that he would grant to us,

74 That being delivered from the hand of our enemies, we may serve him without fear,

75 In holiness and justice before him, all our days.

R. Blessed be the Lord, the God of Israel; he has come to his people.

Alleluia: Acts 16: 14b

R. Alleluia, alleluia.

14b Open our hearts, O Lord, to listen to the words of your Son.

R. Alleluia, alleluia.

Gospel: Luke 11: 5-13

5 And he said to them: Which of you shall have a friend, and shall go to him at midnight, and shall say to him: Friend, lend me three loaves,*6* Because a friend of mine is come off his journey to me, and I have not what to set before him.*7* And he from within should answer, and say: Trouble me not, the door is now shut, and my children are with me in bed; I cannot rise and give thee.*8* Yet if he shall continue knocking, I say to you, although he will not rise and give him, because he is his friend; yet, because of his importunity, he will rise, and give him as many as he needeth.*9* And I say to you, Ask, and it shall be given you: seek, and you shall find: knock, and it shall be opened to you.*10* For every one that asketh, receiveth; and he that seeketh, findeth; and to him that knocketh, it shall be opened.*11* And which of you, if he ask his father bread, will he give him a stone? or a fish, will he for a fish give him a serpent?*12* Or if he shall ask an egg, will he reach him a scorpion?*13* If you then, being evil, know how to give good gifts to your children, how much more will your Father from heaven give the good Spirit to them that ask him?

October 11, 2024

Friday of the Twenty-seventh Week in Ordinary Time

First Reading: Galatians 3: 7-14

7 Know ye therefore, that they who are of faith, the same are the children of Abraham.*8* And the scripture, foreseeing, that God justifieth the Gentiles by faith, told unto Abraham before: In thee shall all nations be blessed.*9* Therefore they that are of faith, shall be blessed with faithful Abraham.*10* For as many as are of the works of the law, are under a curse. For it is written: Cursed is every one, that abideth not in all things, which are written in the book of the law to do them.*11* But that in the law no man is justified with God, it is manifest: because the just man liveth by faith.*12* But the law is not of faith: but, He that doth those things, shall live in them. *13* Christ hath redeemed us from the curse of the law, being made a curse for us: for it is written: Cursed is every one that hangeth on a tree: *14* That the blessing of Abraham might come on the Gentiles through Christ Jesus: that we may receive the promise of the Spirit by faith.

Responsorial Psalm: Psalms 111: 1b-2, 3-4, 5-6

R. (5) The Lord will remember his covenant for ever.

1 I will praise thee, O Lord, with my whole heart; in the council of the just: and in the congregation.

2 Great are the works of the Lord: sought out according to all his wills.

R. The Lord will remember his covenant for ever.

3 His work is praise and magnificence: and his justice continueth for ever and ever.

4 He hath made a remembrance of his wonderful works, being a merciful and gracious Lord:

R. The Lord will remember his covenant for ever.

5 He hath given food to them that fear him. He will be mindful for ever of his covenant:

6 He will shew forth to his people the power of his works.

R. The Lord will remember his covenant for ever.

Alleluia: John 12: 31b-32

R. Alleluia, alleluia.

31b-32 The prince of this world will now be cast out, and when I am lifted up from the earth I will draw all to myself, says the Lord.

R. Alleluia, alleluia.

Gospel: Luke 11: 15-26

15 But some of them said: He casteth out devils by Beelzebub, the prince of devils. *16* And others tempting, asked of him a sign from heaven. *17* But he seeing their thoughts, said to them: Every kingdom divided against itself, shall be brought to desolation, and house upon house shall fall. *18* And if Satan also be divided against himself, how shall his kingdom stand? because you say, that through Beelzebub I cast out devils. *19* Now if I cast out devils by Beelzebub; by whom do your children cast them out? Therefore they shall be your judges. *20* But if I by the finger of God cast out devils; doubtless the kingdom of God is come upon you. *21* When a strong man armed keepeth his court, those things are in peace which he possesseth. *22* But if a stronger than he come upon him, and overcome him; he will take away all his armour wherein he trusted, and will distribute his spoils. *23* He that is not with me, is against me; and he that gathereth not with me, scattereth. *24* When the unclean spirit is gone out of a man, he walketh through places without water, seeking rest; and not finding, he saith: I will return into my house whence I came out. *25* And when he is come, he findeth it swept and garnished. *26* Then he goeth and taketh with him seven other spirits more wicked than himself, and entering in they dwell there. And the last state of that man becomes worse than the first.

October 12, 2024

Saturday of the Twenty-seventh Week in Ordinary Time

First Reading: Galatians 3: 22-29

22 But the scripture hath concluded all under sin, that the promise, by the faith of Jesus Christ, might be given to them that believe.23 But before the faith came, we were kept under the law shut up, unto that faith which was to be revealed.24 Wherefore the law was our pedagogue in Christ, that we might be justified by faith.25 But after the faith is come, we are no longer under a pedagogue.26 For you are all the children of God by faith, in Christ Jesus.27 For as many of you as have been baptized in Christ, have put on Christ.28 There is neither Jew nor Greek: there is neither bond nor free: there is neither male nor female. For you are all one in Christ Jesus.29 And if you be Christ's, then are you the seed of Abraham, heirs according to the promise.

Responsorial Psalm: Psalms 105: 2-3, 4-5, 6-7

R. (8a) The Lord remembers his covenant for ever.

or

R. Alleluia.

2 Sing to him, yea sing praises to him: relate all his wondrous works.

3 Glory ye in his holy name: let the heart of them rejoice that seek the Lord.

R. The Lord remembers his covenant for ever.

or

R. Alleluia.

4 Seek ye the Lord, and be strengthened: seek his face evermore.

5 Remember his marvellous works which he hath done; his wonders, and the judgments of his mouth.

R. The Lord remembers his covenant for ever.

or

R. Alleluia.

6 O ye seed of Abraham his servant; ye sons of Jacob his chosen.

7 He is the Lord our God: his judgments are in all the earth.

R. The Lord remembers his covenant for ever.

or

R. Alleluia.

Alleluia: Luke 11: 28

R. Alleluia, alleluia.

28 Blessed are those who hear the word of God and observe it.

R. Alleluia, alleluia.

Gospel: Luke 11: 27-28

27 And it came to pass, as he spoke these things, a certain woman from the crowd, lifting up her voice, said to him: Blessed is the womb that bore thee, and the paps that gave thee suck.*28* But he said: Yea rather, blessed are they who hear the word of God, and keep it.

October 13, 2024

Twenty-eighth Sunday in Ordinary Time

First Reading: Wisdom 7: 7-11

7 Wherefore I wished, and understanding was given me: and I called upon God, and the spirit of wisdom came upon me:*8* And I preferred her before kingdoms and thrones, and esteemed riches nothing in comparison of her.*9* Neither did I compare unto her any precious stone: for all gold in comparison of her, is as a little sand, and silver in respect to her shall be counted as clay.*10* I loved her above health and beauty, and chose to have her instead of light: for her light cannot be put out.*11* Now all good things came to me together with her, and innumerable riches through her hands,

Responsorial Psalm: Psalms 90: 12-13, 14-15, 16-17

R. (14) Fill us with your love, O Lord, and we will sing for joy!

12 Can number thy wrath? So make thy right hand known: and men learned in heart, in wisdom.

13 Return, O Lord, how long? and be entreated in favour of thy servants.

R. Fill us with your love, O Lord, and we will sing for joy!

14 We are filled in the morning with thy mercy: and we have rejoiced, and are delighted all our days.

15 We have rejoiced for the days in which thou hast humbled us: for the years in which we have seen evils.

R. Fill us with your love, O Lord, and we will sing for joy!

16 Look upon thy servants and upon their works: and direct their children.

17 And let the brightness of the Lord our God be upon us: and direct thou the works of our hands over us; yea, the work of our hands do thou direct.

R. Fill us with your love, O Lord, and we will sing for joy!

Second Reading: Hebrews 4: 12-13

12 For the word of God is living and effectual, and more piercing than any two edged sword; and reaching unto the division of the soul and the spirit, of the joints also and the marrow, and is a discerner of the thoughts and intents of the heart.*13* Neither is there any creature invisible in his sight: but all things are naked and open to his eyes, to whom our speech is.

Alleluia: Matthew 5: 3

R. Alleluia, alleluia.

3 Blessed are the poor in spirit: for theirs is the kingdom of heaven.

R. Alleluia, alleluia.

Gospel: Mark 10: 17-30

17 And when he was gone forth into the way, a certain man running up and kneeling before him, asked him, Good Master, what shall I do that I may receive life everlasting?*18* And Jesus said to him, Why callest thou me good? None is good but one, that is God.*19* Thou knowest the commandments: Do not commit adultery, do not kill, do not steal, bear not false witness, do no fraud, honour thy father and mother.*20* But he answering, said to him: Master, all these things I have observed from my youth.*21* And Jesus looking on him, loved him, and said to him: One thing is wanting unto thee: go, sell whatsoever thou hast, and give to the poor, and thou shalt have treasure in heaven; and come, follow me.*22* Who being struck sad at that saying, went away sorrowful: for he had great possessions.*23* And Jesus looking round about, saith to his disciples: How hardly shall they that have riches, enter into the kingdom of God!*24* And the disciples were astonished at his words. But Jesus again answering, saith to them: Children, how hard is it for them that trust in riches, to enter into the kingdom of God?*25* It is easier for a camel to pass through the eye of a needle, than for a rich man to enter into the kingdom of God.*26* Who wondered the more, saying among themselves: Who then can be saved?*27* And Jesus looking on them, saith: With men it is impossible; but not with God: for all things are possible with God.*28* And Peter began to say unto him: Behold, we have left all things, and have followed thee.*29* Jesus answering, said: Amen I say to you, there is no man who hath left house or brethren, or sisters, or father, or mother, or children, or lands, for my sake and for the gospel,*30* Who shall not receive an hundred times as much, now in this time; houses, and brethren, and sisters, and mothers, and children, and lands, with persecutions: and in the world to come life everlasting.

October 14, 2024

Monday of the Twenty-eighth Week in Ordinary Time

First Reading: Galatians 4: 22-24, 26-27, 31 – 5: 1

22 For it is written that Abraham had two sons: the one by a bondwoman, and the other by a free woman.*23* But he who was of the bondwoman, was born according to the flesh: but he of the free woman, was by promise.*24* Which things are said by an allegory. For these are the two testaments. The one from mount Sina, engendering unto bondage; which is Agar:*26* But that Jerusalem, which is above, is free: which is our mother.*27* For it is written: Rejoice, thou barren, that bearest not: break forth and cry, thou that travailest not: for many are the children of the desolate, more than of her that hath a husband.*31* So then, brethren, we are not the children of the bondwoman, but of the free: by the freedom wherewith Christ has made us free.*5:1* Stand fast, and be not held again under the yoke of bondage.

Responsorial Psalm: Psalms 113: 1b-2, 3-4, 5a and 6-7

R. (2) Blessed be the name of the Lord forever.

or

R. Alleluia.

1 Praise the Lord, ye children: praise ye the name of the Lord.

2 Blessed be the name of the Lord, from henceforth now and for ever.

R. Blessed be the name of the Lord forever.

or

R. Alleluia.

3 From the rising of the sun unto the going down of the same, the name of the Lord is worthy of praise.

4 The Lord is high above all nations; and his glory above the heavens.

R. Blessed be the name of the Lord forever.

or

R. Alleluia.

5 Who is as the Lord our God, who dwelleth on high:

6 And looketh down on the low things in heaven and in earth?

7 Raising up the needy from the earth, and lifting up the poor out of the dunghill:

R. Blessed be the name of the Lord forever.

or

R. Alleluia.

Alleluia: Psalms 95: 8

R. Alleluia, alleluia.

8 If today you hear his voice, harden not your hearts.

R. Alleluia, alleluia.

Gospel: Luke 11: 29-32

29 And the multitudes running together, he began to say: This generation is a wicked generation: it asketh a sign, and a sign shall not be given it, but the sign of Jonas the prophet.30 For as Jonas was a sign to the Ninivites; so shall the Son of man also be

to this generation.*31* The queen of the south shall rise in the judgment with the men of this generation, and shall condemn them: because she came from the ends of the earth to hear the wisdom of Solomon; and behold more than Solomon here.*32* The men of Ninive shall rise in the judgment with this generation, and shall condemn it; because they did penance at the preaching of Jonas; and behold more than Jonas here.

October 15, 2024

Memorial of Saint Teresa of Jesus, Virgin and Doctor of the Church
First Reading: Galatians 5: 1-6

1 Stand fast, and be not held again under the yoke of bondage.*2* Behold, I Paul tell you, that if you be circumcised, Christ shall profit you nothing.*3* And I testify again to every man circumcising himself, that he is a debtor to the whole law.*4* You are made void of Christ, you who are justified in the law: you are fallen from grace.*5* For we in spirit, by faith, wait for the hope of justice.*6* For in Christ Jesus neither circumcision availeth any thing, nor uncircumcision: but faith that worketh by charity.

Responsorial Psalm: Psalms 119: 41, 43, 44, 45, 47, 48

R. (41a) Let your mercy come to me, O Lord.

41 Let thy mercy also come upon me, O Lord: thy salvation according to thy word.

R. Let your mercy come to me, O Lord.

43 And take not thou the word of truth utterly out of my mouth: for in thy words have I hoped exceedingly.

R. Let your mercy come to me, O Lord.

44 So shall I always keep thy law, for ever and ever.

R. Let your mercy come to me, O Lord.

45 And I walked at large: because I have sought after thy commandments.

R. Let your mercy come to me, O Lord.

47 I meditated also on thy commandments, which I loved.

R. Let your mercy come to me, O Lord.

48 And I lifted up my hands to thy commandments, which I loved: and I was exercised in thy justifications.

R. Let your mercy come to me, O Lord.

Alleluia: Hebrews 4: 12

R. Alleluia, alleluia.

12 The word of God is living and effective, able to discern reflections and thoughts of the heart.

R. Alleluia, alleluia.

Gospel: Luke 11: 37-41

37 And as he was speaking, a certain Pharisee prayed him, that he would dine with him. And he going in, sat down to eat.*38* And the Pharisee began to say, thinking within himself, why he was not washed before dinner.*39* And the Lord said to him:

Now you Pharisees make clean the outside of the cup and of the platter; but your inside is full of rapine and iniquity.*40* Ye fools, did not he that made that which is without, make also that which is within?*41* But yet that which remaineth, give alms; and behold, all things are clean unto you.

October 16, 2024

Wednesday of the Twenty-eighth Week in Ordinary Time

First Reading: Galatians 5: 18-25

18 But if you are led by the spirit, you are not under the law.*19* Now the works of the flesh are manifest, which are fornication, uncleanness, immodesty, luxury,*20* Idolatry, witchcrafts, enmities, contentions, emulations, wraths, quarrels, dissensions, sects,*21* Envies, murders, drunkenness, revellings, and such like. Of the which I foretell you, as I have foretold to you, that they who do such things shall not obtain the kingdom of God.*22* But the fruit of the Spirit is, charity, joy, peace, patience, benignity, goodness, longanimity,*23* Mildness, faith, modesty, continency, chastity. Against such there is no law.*24* And they that are Christ's, have crucified their flesh, with the vices and concupiscences.*25* If we live in the Spirit, let us also walk in the Spirit.

Responsorial Psalm: Psalms 1: 1-2, 3, 4 and 6

R. (Jn 8:12) Those who follow you, Lord, will have the light of life.

1 Blessed is the man who hath not walked in the counsel of the ungodly, nor stood in the way of sinners, nor sat in the chair of pestilence.

2 But his will is in the law of the Lord, and on his law he shall meditate day and night.

R. Those who follow you, Lord, will have the light of life.

3 And he shall be like a tree which is planted near the running waters, which shall bring forth its fruit, in due season. And his leaf shall not fall off: and all whatsoever he shall do shall prosper.

R. Those who follow you, Lord, will have the light of life.

4 Not so the wicked, not so: but like the dust, which the wind driveth from the face of the earth.

6 For the Lord knoweth the way of the just: and the way of the wicked shall perish.

R. Those who follow you, Lord, will have the light of life.

Alleluia: John 10: 27

R. Alleluia, alleluia.

27 My sheep hear my voice, says the Lord; I know them, and they follow me.

R. Alleluia, alleluia.

Gospel: Luke 11: 42-46

42 But woe to you, Pharisees, because you tithe mint and rue and every herb; and pass over judgment, and the charity of God. Now these things you ought to have done, and not to leave the other undone.43 Woe to you, Pharisees, because you love the uppermost seats in the synagogues, and salutations in the marketplace.44 Woe to you, because you are as sepulchres that appear not, and men that walk over are not aware.45 And one of the lawyers answering, saith to him: Master, in saying these things, thou reproachest us also.46 But he said: Woe to you lawyers also, because you load men with burdens which they cannot bear, and you yourselves touch not the packs with one of your fingers.

October 17, 2024

Memorial of Saint Ignatius of Antioch, Bishop and Martyr

First Reading: Ephesians 1: 1-10

1 Paul, an apostle of Jesus Christ, by the will of God, to all the saints who are at Ephesus, and to the faithful in Christ Jesus.*2* Grace be to you, and peace from God the Father, and from the Lord Jesus Christ.*3* Blessed be the God and Father of our Lord Jesus Christ, who hath blessed us with spiritual blessings in heavenly places, in Christ:*4* As he chose us in him before the foundation of the world, that we should be holy and unspotted in his sight in charity.*5* Who hath predestinated us unto the adoption of children through Jesus Christ unto himself: according to the purpose of his will:*6* Unto the praise of the glory of his grace, in which he hath graced us in his beloved son.*7* In whom we have redemption through his blood, the remission of sins, according to the riches of his grace,*8* Which hath superabounded in us in all wisdom and prudence,*9* That he might make known unto us the mystery of his will, according to his good pleasure, which he hath purposed in him,*10* In the dispensation of the fulness of times, to re-establish all things in Christ, that are in heaven and on earth, in him.

Responsorial Psalm: Psalms 98: 1, 2-3ab, 3cd-4, 5-6

R. (2a) The Lord has made known his salvation.

1 Sing ye to the Lord a new canticle: because he hath done wonderful things. His right hand hath wrought for him salvation, and his arm is holy.

R. The Lord has made known his salvation.

2 The Lord hath made known his salvation: he hath revealed his justice in the sight of the Gentiles.

3ab He hath remembered his mercy his truth toward the house of Israel.

R. The Lord has made known his salvation.

3cd All the ends of the earth have seen the salvation of our God.

4 Sing joyfully to God, all the earth; make melody, rejoice and sing.

R. The Lord has made known his salvation.

5 Sing praise to the Lord on the harp, on the harp, and with the voice of a psalm:

6 With long trumpets, and sound of comet. Make a joyful noise before the Lord our king:

R. The Lord has made known his salvation.

Alleluia: John 14: 6

R. Alleluia, alleluia.

6 I am the way and the truth and the life, says the Lord; no one comes to the Father except through me.

R. Alleluia, alleluia.

Gospel: Luke 11: 47-54

47 Woe to you who build the monuments of the prophets: and your fathers killed them.*48* Truly you bear witness that you consent to the doings of your fathers: for they indeed killed them, and you build their sepulchres.*49* For this cause also the wisdom of God said: I will send to them prophets and apostles; and some of them they will kill and persecute.*50* That the blood of all the prophets which was shed from the foundation of the world, may be required of this generation,*51* From the blood of Abel unto the blood of Zacharias, who was slain between the alter and the temple: Yea I say to you, It shall be required of this generation.*52* Woe to you lawyers, for you have taken away the key of knowledge: you yourselves have not entered in, and those that were entering in, you have hindered.*53* And as he was saying these things to them, the Pharisees and the lawyers began violently to urge him, and to oppress his mouth about many things,*54* Lying in wait for him, and seeking to catch something from his mouth, that they might accuse him.

October 18, 2024

Feast of Saint Luke, evangelist

First Reading: Second Timothy 4: 10-17b

10 Crescens into Galatia, Titus into Dalmatia.*11* Only Luke is with me. Take Mark, and bring him with thee: for he is profitable to me for the ministry.*12* But Tychicus I have sent to Ephesus.*13* The cloak that I left at Troas, with Carpus, when thou comest, bring with thee, and the books, especially the parchments.*14* Alexander the coppersmith hath done me much evil: the Lord will reward him according to his works:*15* Whom do thou also avoid, for he hath greatly withstood our words.*16* At my first answer no man stood with me, but all forsook me: may it not be laid to their charge.*17* But the Lord stood by me, and strengthened me, that by me the preaching may be accomplished, and that all the Gentiles may hear.

Responsorial Psalm: Psalms 145: 10-11, 12-13, 17-18

R. (12) **Your friends make known, O Lord, the glorious splendor of your Kingdom.**

10 Let all thy works, O lord, praise thee: and let thy saints bless thee.

11 They shall speak of the glory of thy kingdom: and shall tell of thy power:

R. Your friends make known, O Lord, the glorious splendor of your Kingdom.

12 To make thy might known to the sons of men: and the glory of the magnificence of thy kingdom.

13 Thy kingdom is a kingdom of all ages: and thy dominion endureth throughout all generations. The Lord is faithful in all his words: and holy in all his works.

R. Your friends make known, O Lord, the glorious splendor of your Kingdom.

17 The Lord is just in all his ways: and holy in all his works.

18 The Lord is nigh unto all them that call upon him: to all that call upon him in truth.

R. Your friends make known, O Lord, the glorious splendor of your Kingdom.

Alleluia: John 15: 16

R. Alleluia, alleluia.

16 I chose you from the world, to go and bear fruit that will last, says the Lord.

R. Alleluia, alleluia.

Gospel: Luke 10: 1-9

1 And after these things the Lord appointed also other seventy-two: and he sent them two and two before his face into every city and place whither he himself was to come.*2* And he said to them: The harvest indeed is great, but the labourers are few. Pray ye therefore the Lord of the harvest, that he send labourers into his harvest.*3* Go: Behold I send you as lambs among wolves.*4* Carry neither purse, nor scrip, nor shoes; and salute no man by the way.*5* Into whatsoever house you enter, first say: Peace be to this house.*6* And if the son of peace be there, your peace shall rest upon him; but if not, it shall return to you.*7* And in the same house, remain, eating and drinking such things as they have: for the labourer is worthy of his hire. Remove not from house to house.*8* And into what city soever you enter, and they receive you, eat such things as are set before you.*9* And heal the sick that are therein, and say to them: The kingdom of God is come nigh unto you.

October 19, 2024

Memorial of Saints John de Brébeuf and Isaac Jogues, Priests, and Companions, Martyrs

First Reading: Ephesians 1: 15-23

15 Wherefore I also, hearing of your faith that is in the Lord Jesus, and of your love towards all the saints,*16* Cease not to give thanks for you, making commemoration of you in my prayers,*17* That the God of our Lord Jesus Christ, the Father of glory, may give unto you the spirit of wisdom and of revelation, in the knowledge of him:*18* The eyes of your heart enlightened, that you may know what the hope is of the glory of his inheritance in the saints.*19* And what is the exceeding greatness of his power towards us, who believe according to the operation of the might of his power,*20* Which he wrought in Christ, raising him up from the dead, and setting him on his right hand in the heavenly places.*21* Above all principality, and power, and virtue, and dominion, and every name that is named, not only in this world, but also in that which is to come.*22* And he hath subjected all things under his feet, and hath made him head over all the church,*23* Which is his body, and the fulness of him who is filled all in all.

Responsorial Psalm: Psalms 8: 2-3ab, 4-5, 6-7

R. (7) You have given your Son rule over the works of your hands.

2 O Lord our Lord, how admirable is thy name in the whole earth! For thy magnificence is elevated above the heavens.

3ab Out of the mouth of infants and of sucklings thou hast perfected praise, because of thy enemies.

R. You have given your Son rule over the works of your hands.

4 For I will behold thy heavens, the works of thy fingers: the moon and the stars which thou hast founded.

5 What is man that thou art mindful of him? or the son of man that thou visitest him?

R. You have given your Son rule over the works of your hands.

6 Thou hast made him a little less than the angels, thou hast crowned him with glory and honour:

7 And hast set him over the works of thy hands.

R. You have given your Son rule over the works of your hands.

Alleluia: John 15: 26a, 27a

R. Alleluia, alleluia.

26a, 27a The Spirit of truth will testify to me, says the Lord, and you also will testify.

R. Alleluia, alleluia.

Gospel: Luke 12: 8-12

8 And I say to you, Whosoever shall confess me before men, him shall the Son of man also confess before the angels of God. *9* But he that shall deny me before men, shall be denied before the angels of God. *10* And whosoever speaketh a word against the Son of man, it shall be forgiven him: but to him that shall blaspheme against the Holy Ghost, it shall not be forgiven. *11* And when they shall bring you into the synagogues, and to magistrates and powers, be not solicitous how or what you shall answer, or what you shall say; *12* For the Holy Ghost shall teach you in the same hour what you must say.

October 20, 2024

Twenty-ninth Sunday in Ordinary Time

First Reading: Isaiah 53: 10-11

10 And the Lord was pleased to bruise him in infirmity: if he shall lay down his life for sin, he shall see a long-lived seed, and the will of the Lord shall be prosperous in his hand. *11* Because his soul hath laboured, he shall see and be filled: by his knowledge shall this my just servant justify many, and he shall bear their iniquities.

Responsorial Psalm: Psalms 33: 4-5, 18-19, 20, 22

R. (22) Lord, let your mercy be on us, as we place our trust in you.

4 For the word of the Lord is right, and all his works are done with faithfulness.

5 He loveth mercy and judgment; the earth is full of the mercy of the Lord.

R. Lord, let your mercy be on us, as we place our trust in you.

18 Behold the eyes of the Lord are on them that fear him: and on them that hope in his mercy.

19 To deliver their souls from death; and feed them in famine.

R. Lord, let your mercy be on us, as we place our trust in you.

20 Our soul waiteth for the Lord: for he is our helper and protector.

22 Let thy mercy, O Lord, be upon us, as we have hoped in thee.

R. Lord, let your mercy be on us, as we place our trust in you.

Second Reading: Hebrews 4: 14-16

14 Having therefore a great high priest that hath passed into the heavens, Jesus the Son of God: let us hold fast our confession. 15 For we have not a high priest, who can not have compassion on our infirmities: but one tempted in all things like as we are, without sin. 16 Let us go therefore with confidence to the throne of grace: that we may obtain mercy, and find grace in seasonable aid.

Alleluia: Mark 10: 45

R. Alleluia, alleluia.

45 The Son of Man came to serve and to give his life as a ransom for many.

R. Alleluia, alleluia.

Gospel: Mark 10: 35-45 or Mark 10: 42-45

35 And James and John the sons of Zebedee, come to him, saying: Master, we desire that whatsoever we shall ask, thou wouldst do it for us: 36 But he said to them: What would you that I should do for you? 37 And they said: Grant to us, that we may

sit, one on thy right hand, and the other on thy left hand, in thy glory.*38* And Jesus said to them: You know not what you ask. Can you drink of the chalice that I drink of: or be baptized with the baptism wherewith I am baptized?*39* But they said to him: We can. And Jesus saith to them: You shall indeed drink of the chalice that I drink of: and with the baptism wherewith I am baptized, you shall be baptized.*40* But to sit on my right hand, or on my left, is not mine to give to you, but to them for whom it is prepared.*41* And the ten hearing it, began to be much displeased at James and John.*42* But Jesus calling them, saith to them: You know that they who seem to rule over the Gentiles, lord it over them: and their princes have power over them.*43* But it is not so among you: but whosoever will be greater, shall be your minister.*44* And whosoever will be first among you, shall be the servant of all.*45* For the Son of man also is not come to be ministered unto, but to minister, and to give his life a redemption for many.

Or

42 But Jesus calling them, saith to them: You know that they who seem to rule over the Gentiles, lord it over them: and their princes have power over them.*43* But it is not so among you: but whosoever will be greater, shall be your minister.*44* And whosoever will be first among you, shall be the servant of all.*45* For the Son of man also is not come to be ministered unto, but to minister, and to give his life a redemption for many.

October 21, 2024

Monday of the Twenty-ninth Week in Ordinary Time

First Reading: Ephesians 2: 1-10

1 And you, when you were dead in your offences, and sins,*2* Wherein in time past you walked according to the course of this world, according to the prince of the power of this air, of the spirit that now worketh on the children of unbelief:*3* In which also we all conversed in time past, in the desires of our flesh, fulfilling the will of the flesh and of our thoughts, and were by nature children of wrath, even as the rest:*4*

But God, (who is rich in mercy,) for his exceeding charity wherewith he loved us,5 Even when we were dead in sins, hath quickened us together in Christ, (by whose grace you are saved,)6 And hath raised us up together, and hath made us sit together in the heavenly places, through Christ Jesus.7 That he might shew in the ages to come the abundant riches of his grace, in his bounty towards us in Christ Jesus.8 For by grace you are saved through faith, and that not of yourselves, for it is the gift of God;9 Not of works, that no man may glory.10 For we are his workmanship, created in Christ Jesus in good works, which God hath prepared that we should walk in them.

Responsorial Psalm: Psalms 100: 2, 3, 4ab, 4c-5

R. (3b) The Lord made us, we belong to him.

2 Sing joyfully to God, all the earth: serve ye the Lord with gladness. Come in before his presence with exceeding great joy.

R. The Lord made us, we belong to him.

3 Know ye that the Lord he is God: he made us, and not we ourselves. We are his people and the sheep of his pasture.

R. The Lord made us, we belong to him.

4ab Go ye into his gates with praise, into his courts with hymns.

R. The Lord made us, we belong to him.

4c Give glory to him. Praise ye his name.

5 For the Lord is sweet, his mercy endureth for ever, and his truth to generation and generation.

R. The Lord made us, we belong to him.

Alleluia: Matthew 5: 3

R. Alleluia, alleluia.

3 Blessed are the poor in spirit: for theirs is the kingdom of heaven.

R. Alleluia, alleluia.

Gospel: Luke 12: 13-21

13 And one of the multitude said to him: Master, speak to my brother that he divide the inheritance with me.*14* But he said to him: Man, who hath appointed me judge, or divider, over you?*15* And he said to them: Take heed and beware of all covetousness; for a man's life doth not consist in the abundance of things which he possesseth.*16* And he spoke a similitude to them, saying: The land of a certain rich man brought forth plenty of fruits.*17* And he thought within himself, saying: What shall I do, because I have no room where to bestow my fruits?*18* And he said: This will I do: I will pull down my barns, and will build greater; and into them will I gather all things that are grown to me, and my goods.*19* And I will say to my soul: Soul, thou hast much goods laid up for many years take thy rest; eat, drink, make good cheer.*20* But God said to him: Thou fool, this night do they require thy soul of thee: and whose shall those things be which thou hast provided?*21* So is he that layeth up treasure for himself, and is not rich towards God.

October 22, 2024

Tuesday of the Twenty-ninth Week in Ordinary Time

First Reading: Ephesians 2: 12-22

12 That you were at that time without Christ, being aliens from the conversation of Israel, and strangers to the testament, having no hope of the promise, and without God in this world. *13* But now in Christ Jesus, you, who some time were afar off, are made nigh by the blood of Christ. *14* For he is our peace, who hath made both one, and breaking down the middle wall of partition, the enmities in his flesh: *15* Making void the law of commandments contained in decrees; that he might make the two in himself into one new man, making peace; *16* And might reconcile both to God in one body by the cross, killing the enmities in himself. *17* And coming, he preached peace to you that were afar off, and peace to them that were nigh. *18* For by him we have access both in one Spirit to the Father. *19* Now therefore you are no more strangers and foreigners; but you are fellow citizens with the saints, and the domestics of God, *20* Built upon the foundation of the apostles and prophets, Jesus Christ himself being the chief corner stone: *21* In whom all the building, being framed together, groweth up into an holy temple in the Lord. *22* In whom you also are built together into an habitation of God in the Spirit.

Responsorial Psalm: Psalms 85: 9ab-10, 11-12, 13-14

R. (9) The Lord speaks of peace to his people.

9ab I will hear what the Lord God will speak in me: for he will speak peace unto his people.

10 Surely his salvation is near to them that fear him: that glory may dwell in our land.

R. The Lord speaks of peace to his people.

11 Mercy and truth have met each other: justice and peace have kissed.

12 Truth is sprung out of the earth: and justice hath looked down from heaven.

R. The Lord speaks of peace to his people.

13 For the Lord will give goodness: and our earth shall yield her fruit.

14 Justice shall walk before him: and shall set his steps in the way.

R. The Lord speaks of peace to his people.

Alleluia: Luke 21: 36

R. Alleluia, alleluia.

36 Be vigilant at all times and pray that you may have the strength to stand before the Son of Man.

R. Alleluia, alleluia.

Gospel: Luke 12: 35-38

35 Let your loins be girt, and lamps burning in your hands.*36* And you yourselves like to men who wait for their lord, when he shall return from the wedding; that when he cometh and knocketh, they may open to him immediately.*37* Blessed are those servants, whom the Lord when he cometh, shall find watching. Amen I say to you, that he will gird himself, and make them sit down to meat, and passing will minister unto them.*38* And if he shall come in the second watch, or come in the third watch, and find them so, blessed are those servants.

October 23, 2024

Wednesday of the Twenty-ninth Week in Ordinary Time

First Reading: Ephesians 3: 2-12

2 If yet you have heard of the dispensation of the grace of God which is given me towards you:3 How that, according to revelation, the mystery has been made known to me, as I have written above in a few words;4 As you reading, may understand my knowledge in the mystery of Christ,5 Which in other generations was not known to the sons of men, as it is now revealed to his holy apostles and prophets in the Spirit:6 That the Gentiles should be fellow heirs, and of the same body, and co-partners of his promise in Christ Jesus, by the gospel:7 Of which I am made a minister, according to the gift of the grace of God, which is given to me according to the operation of his power:8 To me, the least of all the saints, is given this grace, to preach among the Gentiles, the unsearchable riches of Christ,9 And to enlighten all men, that they may see what is the dispensation of the mystery which hath been hidden from eternity in God, who created all things:10 That the manifold wisdom of God may be made known to the principalities and powers in heavenly places through the church,11 According to the eternal purpose, which he made, in Christ Jesus our Lord:12 In whom we have boldness and access with confidence by the faith of him.

Responsorial Psalm: Isaiah 12: 2-3, 4bcd, 5-6

R. (3) You will draw water joyfully from the springs of salvation.

2 Behold, God is my saviour, I will deal confidently, and will not fear: O because the Lord is my strength, and my praise, and he is become my salvation.

3 You shall draw waters with joy out of the saviour's fountains:

R. You will draw water joyfully from the springs of salvation.

4bcd Praise ye the Lord, and call upon his name: make his works known among the people: remember that his name is high.

R. You will draw water joyfully from the springs of salvation.

5 Sing ye to the Lord, for he hath done great things: shew this forth in all the earth.

6 Rejoice, and praise, O thou habitation of Sion: for great is he that is in the midst of thee, the Holy One of Israel.

R. You will draw water joyfully from the springs of salvation.

Alleluia: Matthew 24: 42a, 44

R. Alleluia, alleluia.

42a, 44 Stay awake! For you do not know when the Son of Man will come.

R. Alleluia, alleluia.

Gospel: Luke 12: 39-48

39 But this know ye, that if the householder did know at what hour the thief would come, he would surely watch, and would not suffer his house to be broken open.40 Be you then also ready: for at what hour you think not, the Son of man will come.41 And Peter said to him: Lord, dost thou speak this parable to us, or likewise to all?42 And the Lord said: Who (thinkest thou) is the faithful and wise steward, whom his lord setteth over his family, to give them their measure of wheat in due season?43 Blessed is that servant, whom when his lord shall come, he shall find so doing.44 Verily I say to you, he will set him over all that he possesseth.45 But if that servant shall say in his heart: My lord is long a coming; and shall begin to strike the menservants and maidservants, and to eat and to drink and be drunk:46 The lord of that servant will come in the day that he hopeth not, and at the hour that he knoweth not, and shall separate him, and shall appoint him his portion with unbelievers.47 And that servant who knew the will of his lord, and prepared not himself, and did not

according to his will, shall be beaten with many stripes.*48* But he that knew not, and did things worthy of stripes, shall be beaten with few stripes. And unto whomsoever much is given, of him much shall be required: and to whom they have committed much, of him they will demand the more.

October 24, 2024

Thursday of the Twenty-ninth Week in Ordinary Time

First Reading: Ephesians 3: 14-21

14 For this cause I bow my knees to the Father of our Lord Jesus Christ,*15* Of whom all paternity in heaven and earth is named,*16* That he would grant you, according to the riches of his glory, to be strengthened by his Spirit with might unto the inward man,*17* That Christ may dwell by faith in your hearts; that being rooted and founded in charity,*18* You may be able to comprehend, with all the saints, what is the breadth, and length, and height, and depth:*19* To know also the charity of Christ, which surpasseth all knowledge, that you may be filled unto all the fulness of God.*20* Now to him who is able to do all things more abundantly than we desire or understand, according to the power that worketh in us;*21* To him be glory in the church, and in Christ Jesus unto all generations, world without end. Amen.

Responsorial Psalm: Psalms 33: 1-2, 4-5, 11-12, 18-19

R. (5b) The earth is full of the goodness of the Lord.

1 Rejoice in the Lord, O ye just: praise becometh the upright.

2 Give praise to the Lord on the harp; sing to him with the psaltery, the instrument of ten strings.

R. The earth is full of the goodness of the Lord.

4 For the word of the Lord is right, and all his works are done with faithfulness.

5 He loveth mercy and judgment; the earth is full of the mercy of the Lord.

R. The earth is full of the goodness of the Lord.

11 But the counsel of the Lord standeth for ever: the thoughts of his heart to all generations.

12 Blessed is the nation whose God is the Lord: the people whom he hath chosen for his inheritance.

R. The earth is full of the goodness of the Lord.

18 Behold the eyes of the Lord are on them that fear him: and on them that hope in his mercy.

19 To deliver their souls from death; and feed them in famine.

R. The earth is full of the goodness of the Lord.

Alleluia: Philippians 3: 8-9

R. Alleluia, alleluia.

8-9 I consider all things so much rubbish that I may gain Christ and be found in him.

R. Alleluia, alleluia.

Gospel: Luke 12: 49-53

49 I am come to cast fire on the earth; and what will I, but that it be kindled?*50* And I have a baptism wherewith I am to be baptized: and how am I straitened until it be accomplished?*51* Think ye, that I am come to give peace on earth? I tell you, no; but separation.*52* For there shall be from henceforth five in one house divided: three against two, and two against three.*53* The father shall be divided against the son, and the son against his father, the mother against the daughter, and the daughter against the mother, the mother in law against her daughter in law, and the daughter in law against her mother in law.

October 25, 2024

Friday of the Twenty-ninth Week in Ordinary Time

First Reading: Ephesians 4: 1-6

1 I therefore, a prisoner in the Lord, beseech you that you walk worthy of the vocation in which you are called,*2* With all humility and mildness, with patience, supporting one another in charity.*3* Careful to keep the unity of the Spirit in the bond of peace.*4* One body and one Spirit; as you are called in one hope of your calling.*5* One Lord, one faith, one baptism.*6* One God and Father of all, who is above all, and through all, and in us all.

Responsorial Psalm: Psalms 24: 1-2, 3-4ab, 5-6

R. (6) Lord, this is the people that longs to see your face.

1 On the first day of the week, a psalm for David. The earth is the Lord's and the fulness thereof: the world, and all they that dwell therein.

2 For he hath founded it upon the seas; and hath prepared it upon the rivers.

R. Lord, this is the people that longs to see your face.

3 Who shall ascend into the mountain of the Lord: or who shall stand in his holy place?

4ab The innocent in hands, and clean of heart, who hath not taken his soul in vain.

R. Lord, this is the people that longs to see your face.

5 He shall receive a blessing from the Lord, and mercy from God his Saviour.

6 This is the generation of them that seek him, of them that seek the face of the God of Jacob.

R. Lord, this is the people that longs to see your face.

Alleluia: Matthew 11: 25

R. Alleluia, alleluia.

25 Blessed are you, Father, Lord of heaven and earth; you have revealed to little ones the mysteries of the Kingdom.

R. Alleluia, alleluia.

Gospel: Luke 12: 54-59

54 And he said also to the multitudes: When you see a cloud rising from the west, presently you say: A shower is coming: and so it happeneth:*55* And when ye see the south wind blow, you say: There will be heat: and it cometh to pass.*56* You hypocrites, you know how to discern the face of the heaven and of the earth: but how is it that you do not discern this time?*57* And why even of yourselves, do you not judge that which is just?*58* And when thou goest with thy adversary to the prince, whilst thou art in the way, endeavour to be delivered from him: lest perhaps he draw thee to the judge, and the judge deliver thee to the exacter, and the exacter cast thee into prison.*59* I say to thee, thou shalt not go out thence, until thou pay the very last mite.

October 26, 2024

Saturday of the Twenty-ninth Week in Ordinary Time

First Reading: Ephesians 4: 7-16

7 But to every one of us is given grace, according to the measure of the giving of Christ.*8* Wherefore he saith: Ascending on high, he led captivity captive; he gave gifts to men.*9* Now that he ascended, what is it, but because he also descended first into the lower parts of the earth?*10* He that descended is the same also that ascended above all the heavens, that he might fill all things.*11* And he gave some apostles, and some prophets, and other some evangelists, and other some pastors and doctors,*12* For the perfecting of the saints, for the work of the ministry, for the edifying of the body of Christ:*13* Until we all meet into the unity of faith, and of the knowledge of the Son of God, unto a perfect man, unto the measure of the age of the fulness of Christ;*14* That henceforth we be no more children tossed to and fro, and carried about with every wind of doctrine by the wickedness of men, by cunning craftiness, by which they lie in wait to deceive.*15* But doing the truth in charity, we may in all things grow up in him who is the head, even Christ:*16* From whom the whole body, being compacted and fitly joined together, by what every joint supplieth, according to the operation in the measure of every part, maketh increase of the body, unto the edifying of itself in charity.

Responsorial Psalm: Psalms 122: 1-2, 3-4ab, 4cd-5

R. (1) Let us go rejoicing to the house of the Lord.

1 I rejoiced at the things that were said to me: We shall go into the house of the Lord.

2 Our feet were standing in thy courts, O Jerusalem.

R. Let us go rejoicing to the house of the Lord.

3 Jerusalem, which is built as a city, which is compact together.

4ab For thither did the tribes go up, the tribes of the Lord.

R. Let us go rejoicing to the house of the Lord.

4cd The testimony of Israel, to praise the name of the Lord.

5 Because their seats have sat in judgment, seats upon the house of David.

R. Let us go rejoicing to the house of the Lord.

Alleluia: Ezekiel 33: 11

R. Alleluia, alleluia.

11 I take no pleasure in the death of the wicked man, says the Lord, but rather in his conversion that he may live.

R. Alleluia, alleluia.

Gospel: Luke 13: 1-9

1 And there were present, at that very time, some that told him of the Galileans, whose blood Pilate had mingled with their sacrifices.*2* And he answering, said to them: Think you that these Galileans were sinners above all the men of Galilee, because they suffered such things?*3* No, I say to you: but unless you shall do penance, you shall all likewise perish.*4* Or those eighteen upon whom the tower fell in Siloe, and slew them: think you, that they also were debtors above all the men that dwelt in Jerusalem?*5* No, I say to you; but except you do penance, you shall all likewise perish.*6* He spoke also this parable: A certain man had a fig tree planted in his vineyard, and he came seeking fruit on it, and found none.*7* And he said to the dresser of the vineyard: Behold, for these three years I come seeking fruit on this fig tree, and I find none. Cut it done therefore: why cumbereth it the ground?*8* But he answering, said to him: Lord, let it alone this year also, until I dig about it, and dung it.*9* And if happily it bear fruit: but if not, then after that thou shalt cut it down.

October 27, 2024

Thirtieth Sunday in Ordinary Time

First Reading: Jeremiah 31: 7-9

7 For thus saith the Lord: Rejoice ye in the joy of Jacob, and neigh before the head of the Gentiles: shout ye, and sing, and say: Save, O Lord, thy people, the remnant of Israel.*8* Behold I will bring them from the north country, and will gather them from the ends of the earth: and among them shall be the blind, and the lame, the woman with child, and she that is bringing forth, together, a great company of them returning hither.*9* They shall come with weeping: and I will bring them back in mercy: and I will bring them through the torrents of waters in a right way, and they shall not stumble in it: for I am a father to Israel, and Ephraim is my firstborn.

Responsorial Psalm: Psalms 126: 1-2, 2-3, 4-5, 6

R. (3) The Lord has done great things for us; we are filled with joy.

1 When the lord brought back the captivity of Sion, we became like men comforted.

2 Then was our mouth filled with gladness; and our tongue with joy.

R. The Lord has done great things for us; we are filled with joy.

2 Then shall they say among the Gentiles: The Lord hath done great things for them.

3 The Lord hath done great things for us: we are become joyful.

R. The Lord has done great things for us; we are filled with joy.

4 Turn again our captivity, O Lord, as a stream in the south.

5 They that sow in tears shall reap in joy.

R. The Lord has done great things for us; we are filled with joy.

6 Going they went and wept, casting their seeds. But coming they shall come with joyfulness, carrying their sheaves.

R. The Lord has done great things for us; we are filled with joy.

Second Reading: Hebrews 5: 1-6

1 For every high priest taken from among men, is ordained for men in the things that appertain to God, that he may offer up gifts and sacrifices for sins:2 Who can have compassion on them that are ignorant and that err: because he himself also is compassed with infirmity.3 And therefore he ought, as for the people, so also for himself, to offer for sins.4 Neither doth any man take the honour to himself, but he that is called by God, as Aaron was.5 So Christ also did not glorify himself, that he might be made a high priest: but he that said unto him: Thou art my Son, this day have I begotten thee.6 As he saith also in another place: Thou art a priest for ever, according to the order of Melchisedech.

Alleluia: Second Timothy 1: 10

R. Alleluia, alleluia.

10 Our Savior Jesus Christ destroyed death and brought life to light through the Gospel.

R. Alleluia, alleluia.

Gospel: Mark 10: 46-52

46 And they came to Jericho: and as he went out of Jericho, with his disciples, and a very great multitude, Bartimeus the blind man, the son of Timeus, sat by the way side begging.*47* Who when he had heard, that it was Jesus of Nazareth, began to cry out, and to say: Jesus son of David, have mercy on me.*48* And many rebuked him, that he might hold his peace; but he cried a great deal the more: Son of David, have mercy on me.*49* And Jesus, standing still, commanded him to be called. And they call the blind man, saying to him: Be of better comfort: arise, he calleth thee.*50* Who casting off his garment leaped up, and came to him.*51* And Jesus answering, said to him: What wilt thou that I should do to thee? And the blind man said to him: Rabboni, that I may see.*52* And Jesus saith to him: Go thy way, thy faith hath made thee whole. And immediately he saw, and followed him in the way.

October 28, 2024

Feast of Saints Simon and Jude, Apostles

First Reading: Ephesians 2: 19-22

19 Now therefore you are no more strangers and foreigners; but you are fellow citizens with the saints, and the domestics of God,*20* Built upon the foundation of the apostles and prophets, Jesus Christ himself being the chief corner stone:*21* In whom all the building, being framed together, groweth up into an holy temple in the Lord.*22* In whom you also are built together into an habitation of God in the Spirit.

Responsorial Psalm: Psalms 19: 2-3, 4-5

R. (5a) Their message goes out through all the earth.

2 The heavens shew forth the glory of God, and the firmament declareth the work of his hands.

3 Day to day uttereth speech, and night to night sheweth knowledge.

R. Their message goes out through all the earth.

4 There are no speeches nor languages, where their voices are not heard.

5 Their sound hath gone forth into all the earth: and their words unto the ends of the world.

R. Their message goes out through all the earth.

Alleluia: See Te Deum

R. Alleluia, alleluia.

We praise you, O God, we acclaim you as Lord; the glorious company of Apostles praise you.

R. Alleluia, alleluia.

Gospel: Luke 6: 12-16

12 And it came to pass in those days, that he went out into a mountain to pray, and he passed the whole night in the prayer of God.13 And when day was come, he

called unto him his disciples; and he chose twelve of them (whom also he named apostles).*14* Simon, whom he surnamed Peter, and Andrew his brother, James and John, Philip and Bartholomew,*15* Matthew and Thomas, James the son of Alpheus, and Simon who is called Zelotes,*16* And Jude, the brother of James, and Judas Iscariot, who was the traitor.

October 29, 2024

Tuesday of the Thirtieth Week in Ordinary Time

First Reading: Ephesians 5: 21-33

21 Being subject one to another, in the fear of Christ.*22* Let women be subject to their husbands, as to the Lord:*23* Because the husband is the head of the wife, as Christ is the head of the church. He is the saviour of his body.*24* Therefore as the church is subject to Christ, so also let the wives be to their husbands in all things.*25* Husbands, love your wives, as Christ also loved the church, and delivered himself up for it:*26* That he might sanctify it, cleansing it by the laver of water in the word of life:*27* That he might present it to himself a glorious church, not having spot or wrinkle, or any; such thing; but that it should be holy, and without blemish.*28* So also ought men to love their wives as their own bodies. He that loveth his wife, loveth himself.*29* For no man ever hated his own flesh; but nourisheth and cherisheth it, as also Christ doth the church:*30* Because we are members of his body, of his flesh, and of his bones.*31* For this cause shall a man leave his father and mother, and shall cleave to his wife, and they shall be two in one flesh.*32* This is a great sacrament; but I speak in Christ and in the church.*33* Nevertheless let every one of you in particular love his wife as himself: and let the wife fear her husband.

Responsorial Psalm: Psalms 128: 1-2, 3, 4-5

R. (1a) Blessed are those who fear the Lord.

1 Blessed are all they that fear the Lord: that walk in his ways.

2 For thou shalt eat the labours of thy hands: blessed art thou, and it shall be well with thee.

R. Blessed are those who fear the Lord.

3 Thy wife as a fruitful vine, on the sides of thy house.

R. Blessed are those who fear the Lord.

4 Behold, thus shall the man be blessed that feareth the Lord.

5 May the Lord bless thee out of Sion: and mayest thou see the good things of Jerusalem all the days of thy life.

R. Blessed are those who fear the Lord.

Alleluia: Matthew 11: 25

R. Alleluia, alleluia.

25 Blessed are you, Father, Lord of heaven and earth; You have revealed to little ones the mysteries of the Kingdom.

R. Alleluia, alleluia.

Gospel: Luke 13: 18-21

18 He said therefore: To what is the kingdom of God like, and whereunto shall I resemble it? 19 It is like to a grain of mustard seed, which a man took and cast into his garden, and it grew and became a great tree, and the birds of the air lodged in the branches thereof. 20 And again he said: Whereunto shall I esteem the kingdom of

God to be like?*21* It is like to leaven, which a woman took and hid in three measures of meal, till the whole was leavened.

October 30, 2024

Wednesday of the Thirtieth Week in Ordinary Time

First Reading: Ephesians 6: 1-9

1 Children, obey your parents in the Lord, for this is just.*2* Honour thy father and thy mother, which is the first commandment with a promise:*3* That it may be well with thee, and thou mayest be long lived upon earth.*4* And you, fathers, provoke not your children to anger; but bring them up in the discipline and correction of the Lord.*5* Servants, be obedient to them that are your lords according to the flesh, with fear and trembling, in the simplicity of your heart, as to Christ:*6* Not serving to the eye, as it were pleasing men, but, as the servants of Christ doing the will of God from the heart,*7* With a good will serving, as to the Lord, and not to men.*8* Knowing that whatsoever good thing any man shall do, the same shall he receive from the Lord, whether he be bond, or free.*9* And you, masters, do the same things to them, forbearing threatenings, knowing that the Lord both of them and you is in heaven; and there is no respect of persons with him.

Responsorial Psalm: Psalms 145: 10-11, 12-13ab, 13cd-14

R. (13c) The Lord is faithful in all his words.

10 Let all thy works, O lord, praise thee: and let thy saints bless thee.

11 They shall speak of the glory of thy kingdom: and shall tell of thy power:

R. The Lord is faithful in all his words.

12 To make thy might known to the sons of men: and the glory of the magnificence of thy kingdom.

13ab Thy kingdom is a kingdom of all ages: and thy dominion endureth throughout all generations.

R. The Lord is faithful in all his words.

13cd The Lord is faithful in all his words: and holy in all his works.

14 The Lord lifteth up all that fall: and setteth up all that are cast down.

R. The Lord is faithful in all his words.

Alleluia: Second Thessalonians 2: 14

R. Alleluia, alleluia.

14 God has called us through the Gospel to possess the glory of our Lord Jesus Christ.

R. Alleluia, alleluia.

Gospel: Luke 13: 22-30

22 And he went through the cities and towns teaching, and making his journey to Jerusalem.*23* And a certain man said to him: Lord, are they few that are saved? But he said to them:*24* Strive to enter by the narrow gate; for many, I say to you, shall seek to enter, and shall not be able.*25* But when the master of the house shall be gone in, and shall shut the door, you shall begin to stand without, and knock at the door, saying: Lord, open to us. And he answering, shall say to you: I know you not, whence you are.*26* Then you shall begin to say: We have eaten and drunk in thy presence, and thou hast taught in our streets.*27* And he shall say to you: I know you not, whence you are: depart from me, all ye workers of iniquity.*28* There shall be weeping and gnashing of teeth, when you shall see Abraham and Isaac and Jacob, and all the prophets, in the kingdom of God, and you yourselves thrust out.*29* And there shall come from the east and the west, and the north and the south; and shall sit down in the kingdom of God.*30* And behold, they are last that shall be first; and they are first that shall be last.

October 31, 2024

Thursday of the Thirtieth Week in Ordinary Time

First Reading: Ephesians 6: 10-20

10 Finally, brethren, be strengthened in the Lord, and in the might of his power.*11* Put you on the armour of God, that you may be able to stand against the deceits of the devil.*12* For our wrestling is not against flesh and blood; but against principalities and power, against the rulers of the world of this darkness, against the spirits of wickedness in the high places.*13* Therefore take unto you the armour of God, that you may be able to resist in the evil day, and to stand in all things perfect.*14* Stand therefore, having your loins girt about with truth, and having on the breastplate of justice,*15* And your feet shod with the preparation of the gospel of peace:*16* In all things taking the shield of faith, wherewith you may be able to extinguish all the fiery darts of the most wicked one.*17* And take unto you the helmet of salvation, and the sword of the Spirit (which is the word of God).*18* By all prayer and supplication praying at all times in the spirit; and in the same watching with all instance and supplication for all the saints:*19* And for me, that speech may be given me, that I may open my mouth with confidence, to make known the mystery of the gospel.*20* For which I am an ambassador in a chain, so that therein I may be bold to speak according as I ought.

Responsorial Psalm: Psalms 144: 1b, 2, 9-10

R. (1b) Blessed be the Lord, my Rock!

1 Blessed be the Lord my God, who teacheth my hands to fight, and my fingers to war.

R. Blessed be the Lord, my Rock!

2 My mercy, and my refuge: my support, and my deliverer: My protector, and I have hoped in him: who subdueth my people under me.

R. Blessed be the Lord, my Rock!

9 To thee, O God, I will sing a new canticle: on the psaltery and an instrument of ten strings I will sing praises to thee.

10 Who givest salvation to kings: who hast redeemed thy servant David from the malicious sword:

R. Blessed be the Lord, my Rock!

Alleluia: Luke 19: 38; 2:14

R. Alleluia, alleluia.

19:38, 2:14 Blessed is the king who comes in the name of the Lord. Glory to God in the highest and on earth peace to those on whom his favor rests.

R. Alleluia, alleluia.

Gospel: Luke 13: 31-35

31 The same day, there came some of the Pharisees, saying to him: Depart, and get thee hence, for Herod hath a mind to kill thee. *32* And he said to them: Go and tell that fox, Behold, I cast out devils, and do cures today and tomorrow, and the third day I am consummated. *33* Nevertheless I must walk today and tomorrow, and the day following, because it cannot be that a prophet perish, out of Jerusalem. *34* Jerusalem, Jerusalem, that killest the prophets, and stonest them that are sent to thee, how often would I have gathered thy children as the bird doth her brood under her wings, and thou wouldest not? *35* Behold your house shall be left to you desolate. And I say to you, that you shall not see me till the time come, when you shall say: Blessed is he that cometh in the name of the Lord.

Made in the USA
Las Vegas, NV
14 September 2024

95279284R00044